Withdrawn

Orangutans

By Mara Grunbaum

Children's Press®

An Imprint of Scholastic Inc.

Content Consultant
Audra Meinelt
Curator, Congo Expedition
Columbus Zoo and Aquarium

Library of Congress Cataloging-in-Publication Data
Names: Grunbaum, Mara, author.
Title: Orangutans/by Mara Grunbaum.
Description: New York, NY: Children's Press, an imprint of Scholastic, Inc.,
2018. | Series: Nature's children | Includes index.
Identifiers: LCCN 2017028059 | ISBN 9780531234815 (library binding) | ISBN 9780531245118 (pbk.)
Subjects: LCSH: Orangutans—Juvenile literature. | Rain forest animals—Juvenile literature.
Classification: LCC QL737.P94 G78 2018 | DDC 599.88/3—dc23
LC record available at https://lccn.loc.gov/2017028059

Design by Anna Tunick Tabachnik

Creative Direction: Judith Christ-Lafond for Scholastic

Produced by Spooky Cheetah Press

Printed in North Mankato, MN, USA   113

SCHOLASTIC, CHILDREN'S PRESS, NATURE'S CHILDREN™, and associated logos
are trademarks and/or registered trademarks of Scholastic Inc.

1 2 3 4 5 6 7 8 9 10 R 27 26 25 24 23 22 21 20 19 18

Scholastic Inc., 557 Broadway, New York, NY 10012.

Photos ©: cover: David Evison/Shutterstock; 1: Dannyphoto80/Dreamstime; 4 leaves and throughout: stockgraphicdesigns.com;
5 top left: all-silhouettes.com; 5 top right: AlonzoDesign/iStockphoto; 5 bottom: ROSLAN RAHMAN/AFP/Getty Images; 6 icon
and throughout: AlonzoDesign/iStockphoto; 7: Thomas Marent/Minden Pictures; 8-9: Tim Laman/National Geographic Creative;
11: Fuse/Getty Images; 12-13: M Smits/Buiten-beeld/age fotostock; 15: Anup Shah/Nature Picture Library; 16-17: Suzi Eszterhas/
Minden Pictures; 18-19: FLPA/David Hosking/age fotostock; 20 top left: Hiroya Minakuchi/age fotostock; 20 top right: Red ivory/
Shutterstock; 20 bottom left: up close with nature/Getty Images; 20 bottom right: S Kennerknecht/age fotostock;
23: Curil Ruoso/age fotostock; 24-25: ROSLAN RAHMAN/AFP/Getty Images; 26-27: Anup Shah/Getty Images; 28: tostphoto/
iStockphoto; 31: ZUMA Press, Inc./Alamy Images; 32-33: Michael Poliza/Getty Images; 35: Jami Tarris/Getty Images; 37: Konrad
Wothe/Minden Pictures; 38-39: Mattias Klum/Getty Images; 40-41: Kemal Jufri/The New York Times/Redux; 42 left: Nadezhda
Bolotina/Dreamstime; 42 center left: Photography by Daniel Frauchiger, Switzerland/Getty Images; 42 center right: GlobalP/
iStockphoto; 42 right: Eric Isselee/Shutterstock; 43 top left: Aaron Amat/Shutterstock; 43 top center left: GlobalP/iStockphoto;
43 top center right: Audra Meinelt; 43 top right: londoneye/iStockphoto; 43 bottom: Dannyphoto80/Dreamstime.

Maps by Jim McMahon.

Table of Contents

Fact File: Orangutans

World Distribution
Islands of Borneo and Sumatra, Southeast Asia

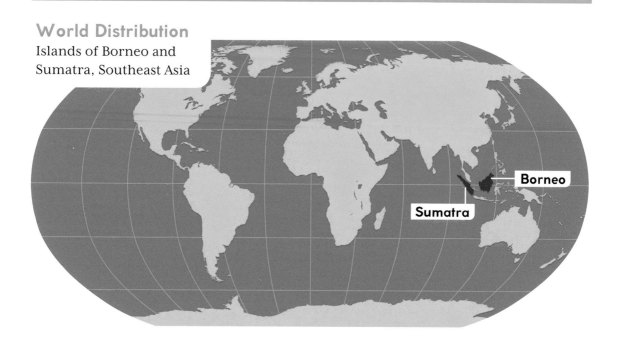

Borneo

Sumatra

Population Status
Critically endangered

Habitats
Tropical forests, including rain forests and swamps

Habits
Live mostly in trees, where they forage for food; communicate with scent, body language, and loud bellows

Diet
Mainly fruits; also leaves, shoots, bark, flowers, nuts, seeds, insects, and bird eggs

Distinctive Features
Shaggy orange-brown hair; extremely long arms; hands and feet that can grip. Some adult males have wide, flat cheek pads called flanges.

Fast Fact
Orangutans are the only great apes that live outside of Africa.

Average Height

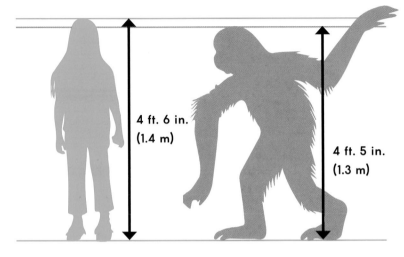

4 ft. 6 in.
(1.4 m)

4 ft. 5 in.
(1.3 m)

Human (age 10)

Orangutan (adult)

Taxonomy

CLASS
Mammalia
(mammals)

ORDER
Primates
(apes, humans,
monkeys, related
animals)

FAMILY
Hominidae
(great apes, humans)

GENUS
Pongo
(orangutans)

SPECIES
- *abelii*
  (Sumatran)
- *pygmaeus*
  (Bornean)

◀ Bornean orangutans
(left) have darker
hair than Sumatran
orangutans.

CHAPTER 1

Endangered Apes

It's morning in the rain forest, and it's quiet among the leaves. Suddenly, there's a rustle in the treetops. A tall trunk begins to sway from side to side. A deep grumble echoes through the branches. Then a loud call: *waaaaaaaaaa-oh!* Two long arms swing. With a flash of reddish-brown hair, an orangutan appears.

Orangutans are apes that make their home in warm, wet forests. They're the largest animals in the world that live entirely in trees.

Thousands of years ago, orangutans lived all over Southeast Asia. Their calls rang out across the rain forest. But today the trees are quieter. Logging, hunting, and other threats have made orangutans **endangered** animals.

Orangutans now live in just two places: the islands of Borneo and Sumatra. The apes on each island are their own **species**. Both could become **extinct** within decades if nothing is done to change their fate.

▶ A baby orangutan stays secure beneath its mother's arm.

Fast Fact
Orangutans can hang upside-down by their feet!

Life in the Trees

Orangutans live in the forest **canopy**. This leafy layer is 60 to 150 feet (18.3 to 45.7 meters) off the ground. The apes spend almost all of their lives in this **habitat**.

An orangutan doesn't jump to get from one tree to another. Instead, it rocks the tree that it's on back and forth. Eventually the tree bends close enough to the tree next to it. Then the orangutan reaches out with its long arms and swings over.

This strategy helps orangutans move through the forest. One orangutan's territory can span up to 4 square miles (10.4 square kilometers). That's an area greater than 1,000 city blocks. The animals move back and forth through the trees across their range as they **forage** for food.

Male orangutans sometimes drop to the ground, where they walk on their hands and feet. But they don't do this for long—the trees are their true home.

◀ An orangutan climbs up a fig tree to reach fruit near the top.

Body Plan

Orangutans have a very distinctive appearance. Their bodies have many **adaptations** suited for life in the trees.

An orangutan's arms are very long in relation to its body. A big male's arms can stretch 8 ft. (2.4 m) from the tips of the fingers on one hand to the tips of the fingers on the other. He can touch his ankles when he's standing up straight! These dangly arms help orangutans swing from tree to tree. These big red apes also have long, curved fingers and toes for gripping branches and vines.

Orangutans have large jaws and strong teeth. This helps them chew fruits and tough plant parts.

These great apes are about 4.3 ft. (1.3 m) tall. They can weigh anywhere from 100 to 250 pounds (45.4 to 113.4 kilograms). Males are much bigger and heavier than females.

Bornean and Sumatran orangutans don't look exactly alike. Sumatran orangutans have thinner faces, lighter hair, and longer beards.

Hook-Shaped Fingers and Toes bend around branches to give orangutans a firm grip.

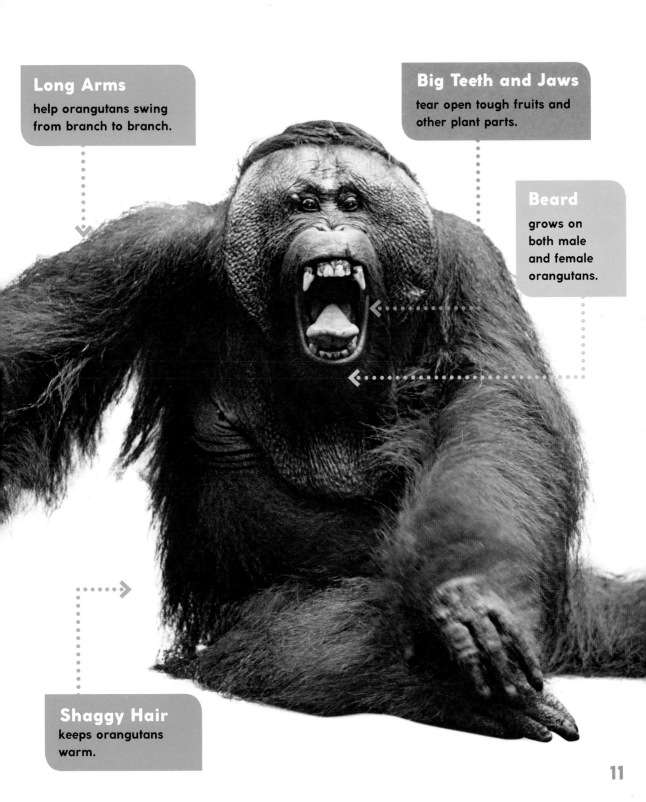

Long Arms
help orangutans swing
from branch to branch.

Big Teeth and Jaws
tear open tough fruits and
other plant parts.

Beard
grows on
both male
and female
orangutans.

Shaggy Hair
keeps orangutans
warm.

11

Fascinating Faces

Orangutans have faces like no other apes. Older males look especially interesting. As they age, the males grow wide, flat pads around their cheeks. These pads are called flanges. They're made of fat under the skin. On Bornean orangutans, flanges curve into a bowl shape.

It can take decades for a male to develop his flanges. Some males never grow them at all. Scientists aren't entirely sure why orangutans have the cheek pads. But they have some ideas. Large flanges may show other orangutans that a male is healthy and strong.

Older males also develop big throat sacs. These pouches hang from their necks. They help the orangutans produce loud, bellowing calls. The calls can be heard almost 1 mi. (1.6 km) away. The sound echoes through the trees, letting everyone in the forest know the orangutan is there.

◀ This male Bornean orangutan has large flanges. Female orangutans prefer males with these cheek pads.

CHAPTER 2

Survival in the Forest

Orangutans make their homes in Borneo and Sumatra. These islands are two of the largest on Earth. They're located on the **equator**, where it stays hot and humid year-round. Between October and March, **monsoons** bring heavy rains. The rain helps thick forests grow on the islands.

The trees provide everything orangutans need to survive. High in the canopy, orangutans find food and shelter. They can even scoop water from holes in the trees. They use their fingers to drip it into their mouths.

In Borneo, adult male orangutans sometimes walk on the ground. But in Sumatra, they don't dare. There, the Sumatran tiger prowls the forest floor. With one false step, an orangutan could become a meal for the big **predator**. Tigers can't climb high, so orangutans stay safe in the trees.

▶ Orangutans eat up to 400 different foods. Tree sap is just one of them.

Fast Fact
Fruits that taste sweet or fatty are orangutans' favorites.

Feasting on Fruit

Orangutans are big animals. And they have big appetites to match. One orangutan can eat more than 20 lb. (9.1 kg) of food in a day. A human, by comparison, eats about 4 lb. (1.8 kg) a day.

Fruits make up most of an orangutan's diet. The apes eat hundreds of different fruits from the rain forest. They especially love the football-sized fruit of the durian tree.

Orangutans may spend seven hours a day foraging for ripe fruits. Sometimes they get lucky. Occasionally an orangutan finds a tree bursting with fruit. Then it settles in for an all-day feast.

At other times, fruits are scarce. Luckily, orangutans are **omnivores**. They can turn to other sources of food, like insects, honey, and even bird eggs. Orangutans may rip off big chunks of tree bark, too. They also snack on tender tree leaves, shoots, and flowers.

◀ Strong teeth help orangutans chew through tough or spiny fruits.

Clever Creatures

Think you could outsmart an orangutan? You should probably think again. Orangutans are very clever animals. They have to be to survive in their forest home!

Orangutans are good at solving problems and learning to do new things. And they have one extra-special talent. Orangutans make tools out of things they find in their habitat. They use sticks to pry open spiky fruits and scrape out the seeds. They also dig insects and honey out of nests. When it rains, they hold leaves over their heads like umbrellas. Not many animals can use objects this way.

Young orangutans learn by copying adults around them. The apes pass their skills from one generation to the next. Like humans, orangutans in different places have different traditions. Some Bornean orangutans use leaves as napkins after eating juicy fruits. In Sumatra, orangutans pile leaves into cushions to sit comfortably in the trees.

▶ When it starts to rain, large palm leaves make a good umbrella.

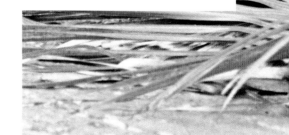

Pygmy Elephant

These miniature Asian elephants live only in the forests of Borneo.

Helmeted Hornbill

▶ These large, hard-headed birds nest high in the trees.

Spiny Turtle

▶ A brown shell helps this spiky reptile blend in with fallen leaves.

Clouded Leopard

This big cat hunts deer and wild pigs on the forest floor.

Nature's Best Gardeners

Scientists often call orangutans "gardeners of the forest." And that's not just because the apes pick so many fruits. Orangutans also keep the forest healthy by helping new trees grow.

The seeds of many fruits are hard to digest. When orangutans spit them out, many of these seeds fall to the ground. If conditions are right, some of them take root. They grow into new rain forest trees.

Orangutans eat fruits from many different types of trees. By dropping the seeds, they help replant the whole forest. This gives them an important job in the **ecosystem**. The trees they start provide a habitat for other animals.

Many animals, from enormous elephants to tiny termites, live in the Asian rain forest. Thousands of species depend on the trees to survive. Many of them, like orangutans, exist nowhere else on Earth. A number of these animals are already endangered. Without orangutans to keep the forest growing, they wouldn't stand a chance.

◄ Orangutans keep the rain forest growing. Species that share their habitat also rely on the forest to survive.

CHAPTER 3

Growing Up Orangutan

Life as an orangutan is never boring.
From finding food to making shelter, there's always
something to do. And female orangutans have another job
that keeps them busy. They tend to their young.

Orangutans **reproduce** very slowly compared to most
animals. A female has just one baby every six to eight
years. She can raise four or five offspring over her lifetime.
That's not many for a **mammal**. Like a human parent, an
orangutan is pregnant for nine months. And she spends
a lot of time caring for each of her young. An orangutan
stays close to its mother until it's around 8 years old.

Orangutans can live up to 40 years in the wild.
In captivity, they've lived even longer. But this slow way of
life has downsides. Because the apes have so few babies,
it takes a long time for the population to grow.

▶ An orangutan mother
keeps watch as her baby
learns to climb.

Mom Knows Best

For the first year of its life, a young orangutan sticks with its mother. Infants cling tightly to their moms' bodies. They hold on to her hair with their hands and feet. Staying close helps keep a baby safe from predators like pythons. These big snakes can't catch adult orangutans. But an infant would be easy **prey**.

After a year, a young orangutan can start to explore on its own. But it still stays near its mother. She carries it when she moves from tree to tree. The mother also continues to **nurse** the baby until it's about three years old.

Living with mom has benefits besides protection. An orangutan mother teaches her young everything it needs to know to live in the trees. By watching her, a young orangutan learns where to find food and how to eat it. It must follow her example if it's going to survive on its own.

◀ A newborn orangutan gets a piggyback ride from its mother.

25

Making the Bed

Young orangutans learn lots of skills. But one is particularly impressive. An orangutan's mother teaches it how to build the perfect treetop nest. These nests keep orangutans warm and cozy while they sleep at night.

Every evening, a mother orangutan climbs 35 to 80 ft. (10.7 to 24.4 m) up a tree. She bends big branches to make a stable platform. Then she adds a soft leafy layer. She weaves in more branches to make the structure strong. Finally, she may make twigs into a pillow and blanket. Now she and her baby can get a good night's sleep.

Orangutans start practicing building nests when they're very young. By age three, they can start sleeping on their own. An orangutan will build thousands of nests in its lifetime. Every morning, the animals abandon their sleeping spots. They construct a new nest from scratch every night.

▶ Orangutans sometimes reuse old nests as napping spots during the day.

Leaving Home

By the age of eight, an orangutan is ready to strike out on its own. By now, the growing animal needs a lot of food. If it kept foraging in the same trees as its mother, neither of them would get enough. The young ape needs to find a territory for itself.

Female orangutans may still visit their mothers occasionally. And at 15 or 16, they start having babies of their own. Sometimes they forage near other females so that their young can meet and play.

Males are much less social. After they leave their mothers, they live almost entirely alone. If two adult males meet, they try to scare each other away. They stare at each other and make threatening calls. They shake trees to show their strength. If neither one gives in, they fight.

These fights can be brutal. But males do it for a reason. The winners mate with nearby females, starting the orangutan life cycle anew.

◀ A big male orangutan is strong enough to break a tall rain forest tree.

CHAPTER 4

All in the Family

In the 1800s, fossils **were discovered** in northern India. They were between 7 million and 13 million years old. The fossils came from an ancient ape.

Scientists named the extinct ape *Sivapithecus*. As more fossils emerged, a clearer picture formed. *Sivapithecus* had a strong jaw, a bowl-shaped face, and large chewing teeth. That made it similar to orangutans today. Scientists think *Sivapithecus* was the **ancestor** of modern orangutans.

Around 300,000 years ago, another orangutan relative roamed the land. *Gigantopithecus* stood up to 10 ft. (3 m) tall. It weighed up to 1,100 lb. (499 kg). It's thought to be the largest ape that ever lived. But *Gigantopithecus* also became extinct. The apes may have run out of food or been hunted by early humans.

Sivapithecus and *Gigantopithecus* lived all over Asia. But modern orangutans live only in Borneo and Sumatra. They're the only apes of their kind left on Earth.

▶ *Gigantopithecus* was more than twice as tall as modern orangutans.

Fast Fact
Great apes are
the largest of
all primates.

Close Cousins

Orangutans' closest living relatives are gorillas, bonobos, chimpanzees, and humans. They are the great apes.

Great apes have much in common. Like all mammals, they have hair and nurse their young. They also have big brains, wide chests, flexible arms, and **opposable** thumbs. All great apes inherited these features from a shared ancestor. That ancestor lived 14 million years ago.

There are many differences between great apes, too. Gorillas, chimpanzees, and bonobos have darker hair than orangutans. At up to 600 lb. (272.2 kg), gorillas are the largest of the great apes. And other great apes are more social than orangutans.

Orangutans are the only great apes that live entirely in trees. Chimpanzees and bonobos spend more time on the ground, and gorillas hardly climb at all. Besides humans, orangutans are the only great apes in Asia. Gorillas, chimpanzees, and bonobos all live in Africa. But like orangutans, they are also endangered.

◀ This gorilla and chimpanzee live together at a mammal orphanage in Africa.

Almost Human

Scientists haven't always known exactly how humans and orangutans are related. But people could always tell that orangutans are similar to us. In fact, that's how they got the name orangutan. It means "person of the forest" in the Malay language of Southeast Asia.

Orangutans are our closest relatives after chimpanzees, bonobos, and gorillas. They share 97 percent of our DNA. And it shows in their many humanlike qualities. Orangutans can stand upright and use tools. They even show emotions on their faces, much as people do.

Humans and orangutans have a long and complicated relationship. Early humans hunted and ate the apes. That drove orangutans to extinction in many areas where they once lived. In the 1700s, European explorers captured orangutans. They brought them home to Europe and put them on display. People were fascinated by the orangutans. But the animals were not treated well. It was not a good life.

Over time, scientists came to understand orangutans better. But unfortunately, threats from humans continue to this day.

▶ Orangutans occasionally walk on two legs, just like people.

CHAPTER 5

A Future Under Threat

Orangutans and their ancestors have lived in Asia for millions of years. But the big red apes may not be there forever. Many problems have made it harder for orangutans to survive. These threats include habitat loss, **climate change**, and illegal hunting.

In the early 1900s, there were 315,000 orangutans in Southeast Asia. Now fewer than 70,000 are left on Earth.

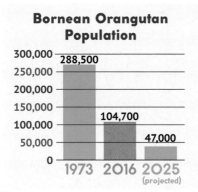

Bornean Orangutan Population

(Source: www.iucnredlist.org/details/full/17975/O)

In 2000, scientists declared Sumatran orangutans critically endangered. That means they may die out in the wild soon. In 2016, Bornean orangutans became critically endangered, too. Recovery can still be possible, though.

▶ **Young orangutans may end up in captivity when they can no longer live in the forest.**

Fast Fact
Borneo is the
third-largest island
in the world.

A Vanishing Home

Deforestation is the most serious threat facing orangutans. People are cutting down forests where the apes live. The land is used for roads, farms, and homes.

In many areas, people have cut down forests to make plantations. They grow trees called oil palms. Oil from these trees is used in foods and household products. Orangutans and other animals are chased off plantations.

Wildfires are another problem. Every few years, a warm climate pattern called **El Niño** occurs. It makes Borneo and Sumatra unusually hot and dry. Fires can rip through the forest. They injure orangutans and burn down the trees where they live.

Over the past few decades, orangutans have lost 80 percent of their habitat. Officials in Borneo and Sumatra want to save what's left. To do that, they've created natural **reserves**. Logging and many other activities are banned in these forest reserves. Orangutans and other animals can live there in peace.

◀ Logging in this area of Borneo has destroyed many rain forest trees.

Learning to Live

Without enough habitat, orangutans can starve. When that happens, they may leave offspring behind. Poachers also kill orangutan mothers and sell the cute babies as pets.

Officials rescue orphaned orangutans when they can. They bring them to **rehabilitation** centers. Veterinarians there nurse the animals back to health. Caretakers feed and cuddle the babies as their mothers would.

The orangutans grow up at the centers. Every day, their human caretakers bring them to "forest school." Forest school is a safe wooded area. The apes can practice finding food and building nests. Human teachers and older orangutans show the young ones what to do.

Orangutans graduate from forest school at age seven or eight. By then, they've learned to survive in the wild. Their caretakers take them to a protected forest and set them free. Life for these young orangutans won't always be easy. But with people around the world fighting for them, they may just stand a chance.

▶ A worker uses a wheelbarrow to take young orangutans to the forest to play.

Orangutan Family Tree

This diagram shows how orangutans are related to other primates. The closer together two animals are on the tree, the more similar they are.

Gibbons
medium-sized, tree-dwelling apes

Monkeys
long-tailed primates that live in trees or on the ground

Tarsiers
tiny primates with extremely large eyes

Lemurs
medium-sized primates that leap from tree to tree

Ancestor of all Primates

Note: Animal photos are not to scale.

Chimpanzees
great apes that
can climb
or walk on
all fours

Bonobos
the last great apes
discovered

Gorillas
the largest
of the
great apes

Humans
apes that walk
on two legs
and have little
body hair

Orangutans
great apes that dwell
almost exclusively
in trees

Words to Know

A .... **adaptations** *(ad-ap-TAY-shuns)* changes a living thing goes through so it fits in better within its environment

ancestor *(ANN-ses-tur)* a family member who lived long ago

C .... **canopy** *(KAN-uh-pee)* the upper layer of a rain forest, consisting mostly of branches, vines, and leaves

climate change *(KLYE-mat chaynj)* global warming and other changes in weather and weather patterns that are happening because of human activity

D .... **DNA** *(DEE-en-AY)* the molecule that carries our genes, found inside the nucleus of cells

E .... **ecosystem** *(EE-koh-sis-tuhm)* all the living things in a place and their relation to their environment

El Niño *(el NEEN-yo)* warm water temperatures, currents, and wind conditions in the Pacific Ocean that affect weather conditions over much of Earth

endangered *(en-DAYN-juhrd)* a plant or animal that is in danger of becoming extinct, usually because of human activity

equator *(i-KWAY-tur)* an imaginary line around the middle of Earth that is an equal distance between the North and South Poles

extinct *(ik-STINGKT)* no longer found alive

F .... **forage** *(FOR-ij)* to go in search of food

fossils *(FAH-suhls)* bones, shells, or other traces of an animal or plant from millions of years ago, preserved as rock

H.......... **habitat** *(HAB-i-tat)* the place where an animal or plant is usually found

M.......... **mammal** *(MAM-uhl)* a warm-blooded animal that has hair or fur and usually gives birth to live babies; female mammals produce milk to feed their young

monsoons *(mahn-SOONS)* very strong winds that occur in different parts of the world; in summer the winds blow from the ocean, causing heavy rains; in winter they blow toward the ocean, creating hot, dry weather

N.......... **nurse** *(NURS)* to feed a baby milk from a breast

O.......... **omnivores** *(AHM-nuh-vorz)* animals or people that eat both plants and meat

opposable *(uh-POZE-uh-buhl)* able to bend to touch other fingers on the same hand

P.......... **predator** *(PRED-uh-tuhr)* an animal that lives by hunting other animals for food

prey *(PRAY)* an animal that is hunted by another animal for food

R.......... **rehabilitation** *(ree-huh-bill-ih-TAY-shun)* the process of bringing an animal back to health

reproduce *(ree-pruh-DOOS)* to produce offspring or individuals of the same kind

reserves *(ri-ZURVZ)* protected places where hunting is not allowed and where animals can live and breed safely

S.......... **species** *(SPEE-sheez)* one of the groups into which animals and plants are divided; members of the same species can mate and have offspring

Find Out More

BOOKS

- Eszterhas, Suzi. *Orangutan Orphanage*. Toronto, Ontario: Owlkids Books Inc., 2016.
- Silverman, Buffy. *Orangutans*. Chicago: Heinemann Library, 2012.
- Taylor, Barbara. *Apes and Monkeys*. New York: Kingfisher, 2011.

WEB PAGES

- www.pbs.org/wnet/nature/orangutans-just-hangin-on-introduction/2266/
  The PBS *Nature* documentary episode "Orangutans, Just Hangin' On," and its companion Web site explore the world of orangutans.
- www.ypte.org.uk/factsheets/orangutan/overview
  The Web site of the Young People's Trust for the Environment (a U.K. charity) provides information about orangutans.
- www.orangutan.org
  The Orangutan Foundation International Web site includes news reports on primate conservation efforts and concerns; information on primate classification, behavior, and natural history; and pertinent links.

Facts for Now

Visit this Scholastic Web site for more information on orangutans:
www.factsfornow.scholastic.com Enter the keyword Orangutan

Index

Index *(continued)*

About the Author

Mara Grunbaum is a science writer and the editor of Scholastic's *SuperScience* magazine. She's fascinated by all animals, from wild orangutans to her domestic cat, Zadie. She lives in Brooklyn, New York.